Grammar Notes

for English Speaking Students

Annalisa Rossi – Maria Giovanna Socci

NUOVA EDIZIONE

Le Monnier

www.lemonnier.it

DIREZIONE EDITORIALE

Franco Ghilardi

REALIZZAZIONE

Redazione e impaginazione: Elisabetta Zappia
Progetto grafico: Patrizia Innocenti

COPERTINA

Progetto grafico e realizzazione: Patrizia Innocenti

Prima edizione: gennaio 2002

Ristampa:

5   2004 2005 2006

La realizzazione di un libro comporta per l'Autore e la redazione
un attento lavoro di revisione e controllo sulle informazioni
contenute nel testo, sull'iconografia e sul rapporto
che intercorre tra testo e immagine.
Nonostante il costante perfezionamento delle procedure di controllo,
sappiamo che è quasi impossibile pubblicare un libro
del tutto privo di errori o refusi.
Per questa ragione ringraziamo fin d'ora i lettori che li vorranno indicare
alla Casa Editrice, al seguente indirizzo:

Via A. Meucci, 2
50015 Grassina (Firenze)
Fax 055.64.91.286
www.lemonnier.it

Nell'eventualità che passi antologici, citazioni o illustrazioni di competenza altrui siano riprodotti in questo volume, l'editore è a disposizione degli aventi diritto che non si sono potuti reperire. L'editore porrà inoltre rimedio, in caso di cortese segnalazione, a eventuali non voluti errori e/o omissioni nei riferimenti relativi.

La Tipografica Varese S.p.A. – Stabilimento di Firenze

INDICE

NOMI E AGGETTIVI, pp. 20-25-247

Most Italian nouns and adjectives end with a vowel.

Masculine nouns and adjectives end in -o in the singular and in -i in the plural.

Questo ragazzo è americano	This boy is American
Questi ragazzi sono americani	These boys are American

Feminine nouns and adjectives end in -a in the singular and in -e in the plural.

Questa ragazza è italiana	This girl is Italian
Queste ragazze sono italiane	These girls are Italian

There is also a group of nouns and adjectives ending in -e in the singular and -i in the plural; they are masculine and feminine. Their gender must be memorized.

Questo giornale	This newspaper
Questi giornali	These newspapers
Questa chiave	This key
Queste chiavi	These keys
Questo ragazzo inglese	This English boy
Questi ragazzi inglesi	These English boys
Questa ragazza francese	This French girl
Queste ragazze francesi	These French girls

Nouns ending with a consonant are usually of foreign origin. They are generally masculine and do not change in the plural.

Questo film	This film
Questi film	These films

Nouns ending with an accented vowel do not change in the plural (see p. 247).

Questa città	This town
Queste città	These towns

Feminine nouns and adjectives ending in the singular in -ca and -ga have their plural in -che and -ghe.

amica	friend (f.)
amiche	friends (f.p.)
larga	large
larghe	large

> NOTE *The adjectives always agree in gender and number with the noun it refers to and usually follow the noun.*

ARTICOLO INDETERMINATIVO, pp. 22-49

The **articolo indeterminativo** (indefinite articles *a-an*) is used only with singular nouns. It has four forms.

Un in front of masculine nouns beginning with a vowel or a consonant.

un libro	a book
un armadio	a wardrobe

Uno in front of masculine nouns beginning with **s + consonant** or **z** or **ps**.

uno sbaglio	a mistake
uno zaino	a rucksack
uno psicologo	a psychologist

Una in front of feminine nouns beginning with a consonant.

una matita	a pencil
una stanza	a room

Un' in front of feminine nouns beginning with a vowel.

un'università	an university
un'agenda	a diary

As the plural of the indefinite article (*some-any*) you can use the preposition **di + the definite article** (*il-lo-la-i-gli-le*) or just omit it. (see pp. 39-49)

(**delle**) sedie	some chairs
(**dei**) tavoli	some tables

ARTICOLO DETERMINATIVO, pp. 25-39-49

The **articolo determinativo** (definite article *the*), as with the indefinite article, precedes the noun to which it refers and agrees with it in gender and number. It has eight forms.

Il in front of masculine nouns beginning with a consonant. Its plural is **i**.

il letto	the bed
i letti	the beds

Lo in front of masculine nouns beginning with **s + consonant** or **z** or **ps**. Its plural is **gli**.

lo specchio	the mirror	**lo** psicologo	the psychologist
gli specchi	the mirrors	**gli** psicologi	the psychologists

L' in front of **masculine nouns beginning with a vowel**. Its plural is gli.

l'armadio	the wardrobe	l'ospedale	the hospital	l'esame	the exam
gli armadi	the wardrobes	gli ospedali	the hospitals	gli esami	the exams

La in front **of feminine nouns beginning with a consonant**. Its plural is le.

la sedia	the chair
le sedie	the chairs

L' in front of **feminine nouns beginning with a vowel**. Its plural is le.

l'aula	the classroom	l'insalata	the salad
le aule	the classrooms	le insalate	the salads

ESSERE, pp. 20-25

The verb **essere** (*to be*) has proper forms in the present indicative.

(io) **Sono** in Italia	I am in Italy
(noi) **Siamo** in Italia	We are in Italy

The expressions **c'è/ci sono** (*there is/there are*), see p. 39, have to be used to indicate that someone or something is in a given place.

In camera **c'è** l'armadio	In the bedroom there is the wardrobe
In camera **ci sono** gli armadi	In the bedroom there are the wardrobes

AVERE, pp. 20-25

The verb **avere** (*to have*) has proper forms in the present indicative and as in English it means possession.

(io) **Ho** un amico tedesco	I have a German friend

It is used also in different expressions:

avere freddo	to be cold
avere caldo	to be hot
avere sete	to be thirsty
avere fame	to be hungry
avere sonno	to be sleepy
avere paura di	to be afraid of
avere voglia di	to wish, to feel like
avere bisogno di	to need
avere... anni	to be...years old
avere mal di...	to have... ache

Laura ha fame	Laura is hungry
Ho venti anni	I am 20 years old
Jim ha sonno	Jim is sleepy
Tu hai bisogno di una penna	You need a pen
Hanno voglia di uscire	They wish to go out
Noi abbiamo caldo	We are hot

FORMA DI CORTESIA E FORMA FAMILIARE, pp. 17-18

In Italian the familiar form tu + the verb in the second person singular is used to address close friends, relatives, children and animals.

The formal form or polite Lei (for masculine and feminine) + the verb in the third person is used to address people you don't know and those with a title. Usually Lei is capitalized.

John, tu sei di Londra?	John, are you from London?
Signora Servadio, (Lei) è di Madrid?	Mrs. Servadio, are you from Madrid?
Ingrid hai una penna?	Ingrid, do you have a pen?
Professore, ha una penna?	Professor, do you have a pen?

> NOTE *In English the subject pronouns are always used with the verb forms. In Italian the verb form itself identifies the subject, so subject pronouns are usually not expressed; they are used to add emphasis or to clarify the subject.*

VERBI - PRESENTE INDICATIVO, pp. 36-49

Italian verbs are organized in three conjugations according to the ending of the infinitive.

Verbs of the first conjugation end in -are.

abitare   to live

Verbs of the second conjugation end in -ere.

scrivere   to write

Verbs of the third conjugation end in -ire.

aprire   to open

All regular verbs of each conjugation are conjugated as the model verb.
The presente indicativo (*present indicative*) of regular verbs is formed by dropping the ending of the infinitive form and adding to the stem the different endings appropriate to the different subjects.

PRIMA CONIUGAZIONE, pp. 36-49

abitare   to live

(io) Abito in Italia   I live in Italy

Verbs ending in -ciare and -giare like *cominciare* (*to begin*), *mangiare* (*to eat*) have one -i in the second person singular and in the first person plural.

(tu) Cominci   You begin
(noi) Mangiamo   We eat

Verbs ending in -care and -gare like *cercare* (*to look for*) or *pagare* (*to pay*) have an -h- before the -i of the second person singular and the first person plural in order to retain the hard sound of -c- and -g-.

(tu) Cerchi la penna   You look for the pen
(noi) Paghiamo l'affitto   We pay the rent

SECONDA CONIUGAZIONE, pp. 36-49

scrivere   to write

(lui) Scrive una lettera   He writes a letter

TERZA CONIUGAZIONE, pp. 36-49

aprire   to open

(loro) Aprono il libro   They open the book

The third conjugation has also a group of verbs like **finire** (*to finish*) that place -isc- between the stem and the ending of the first, second and third persons singular and of the third person plural (see pp. 36-49).

(io) Finisco i compiti	I'll finish homework
(tu) Finisci di lavorare	you'll finish working
(lui-lei) Finisce di studiare	he/she'll finish studying
(noi) Finiamo il lavoro	we'll finish our work
(voi) Finite gli esercizi	you'll finish the exercises
(loro) Finiscono di mangiare	they'll finish eating

These verbs are indicated in the dictionary as (isc)verbs: *preferire* (*to prefer*), *capire* (*to understand*), *pulire* (*to clean*), *spedire* (*to send, to mail*).

NOTE *The presente indicativo (io abito) corresponds to the present (*I live*), present progressive (*I am living*) and present emphatic (*I do live*) tenses in English and it is very often used in place of the future tense.*

In Italian the negative sentence is made up of non in front of the verb.

(io) Non abito in Italia   *I don't live in Italy*

In Italian the interrogative sentence has no inversion or special forms. The use of the question mark with a rising tone of voice on the last word is enough.

Abiti in Italia?   *Do you live in Italy?*

VERBI IRREGOLARI, pp. 57-65-68-69

There are irregular verbs, verbs which do not follow the regular patterns.

In the First Conjugation there are four irregular verbs:

(see p. 57)

andare   to go

Vado a lezione   I go to class
Andiamo dal dottore   We go to the doctor's

(see p. 65)

fare   to do-to make

Faccio gli esercizi   I do homework
Luisa **fa** il caffè   Luisa makes coffee

> **NOTE** *The verb fare is used in many idiomatic expressions where English uses other verbs:*
>
> | | | | |
> | --- | --- | --- | --- |
> | *fare colazione* | to have breakfast | *fare le ore piccole* | to stay up until wee hours |
> | *fare domande* | to ask questions | *fare spese* | to do (the) shopping |
> | *fare fotografie* | to take pictures | *fare un viaggio* | to take a journey |
> | *fare ginnastica* | to exercise | *fare una gita* | to take a trip |
> | *fare il bagno* | to take a bath | *fare una passeggiata* | to take a walk |
> | *fare il bucato* | to do laundry | *fare una pausa* | to have a break |
> | *fare la doccia* | to take a shower | *fare uno spuntino* | to have a snack |
> | *fare la spesa* | to do grocery shopping | | |

(see p. 68)

stare   to stay-to be

Sto bene   I'm fine
Stanno a casa   They stay at home

dare   to give

(io) **do**
I give
(tu) **dai**   un esame
you give   an exam

(lui/lei) **dà**
he/she gives   una festa
(noi) **diamo**   a party
we give

(voi) **date**
you give   un libro a Pietro
(loro) **danno**   a book to Pietro
they give

In the Second Conjugation there are several irregular verbs such as *rimanere* (*io rimango, tu rimani, lei rimane, noi rimaniamo, voi rimanete, loro rimangono*):

Io **rimango** in ufficio fino alle diciassette   I stay/remain in the office until 5 p.m.

There is also a group of three verbs: **volere** (*to want*), **dovere** (*must-to have to*), **potere** (*can-may-to be able*) that are irregular and are called "semiauxiliary verbs" because they are followed by verbs always in the infinitive form (see p. 69).

Voglio un caffè	I want a coffee
Voglio parlare italiano	I want to speak Italian
Devo partire presto	I must leave early
Posso chiudere la finestra?	Can/May I close the window?

In the Third Conjugation there are several irregular verbs such as:

(see. p. 57)

venire   to come

Da dove **vieni**?	Where do you come from?
Vengo da Los Angeles	I come from Los Angeles

(see. p. 57)

uscire   to go out-to leave

Esco ogni sera con gli amici	I go out with friends every night
Escono dalla stanza	They leave the room

dire   to say-to tell

(io) **dico**
I say-tell

(tu) **dici**
you say-tell

     la verità
     the truth

(lui-lei) **dice**
he/she says-tells

(noi) **diciamo**
we say-tell

     qualcosa a Paolo
     something to Paolo

(voi) **dite**
you say-tell

(loro) **dicono**
they say-tell

     di sì
     yes

PASSATO PROSSIMO, pp. 78-86-90

The **passato prossimo** (*present perfect*) is the past tense of a verb used to express an action developed and completed in the past. It is made of the present tense of the auxiliary verbs **avere** (*to have*) or **essere** (*to be*) + **the past participle** of the main verb representing the action.

Ieri sera **ho mangiato** la pizza	Last night I ate pizza
Ieri Anna **è andata** al museo	Yesterday Anna went to the museum

There is no specific rule to choose the **auxiliary verb** *avere* or *essere* to form the **passato prossimo**. With some verbs (mostly) you use the auxiliary verb **avere** conjugated in the present tense (see p. 78).

	Ho parlato italiano		I spoke Italian
	Hai ripetuto l'esercizio		You repeated the exercise
ieri	**Hanno** capito la domanda	yesterday	They understood the question
	Ha viaggiato in treno		They travelled by train
	Abbiamo camminato molto		We walked a lot

With other verbs you use the auxiliary verbs **essere** conjugated in the present tence (see p. 78).

Marco **è** partito ieri	Marco left yesterday
Luisa **è** arrivata due giorni fa	Luisa arrived two days ago
Siamo venuti in treno	We came by train
Luisa e Carla **sono** rimaste a casa	Luisa and Carla remained/stayed at home

> **NOTE** *When you use the auxiliary verb* essere *the past participle agrees in gender and number with the subject.*
>
> *(io)* **Sono** *arrivato/a ieri*   *I arrived yesterday*
> *(noi)* **Siamo** *arrivati/e ieri*   *We arrived yesterday*

The **participio passato** (*past participle*) is formed by adding the appropriate endings to the stem of the infinitive (see p. 90).

Infinitive Verbs in -are	Past Participle -ato
parlare → to speak	parlato spoken

Infinitive Verbs in -ere	Past Participle -uto
ripetere → to repeat	ripetuto repeated

Infinitive Verbs in -ire	Past Participle -ito
capire → to understand	capito understood

Here is a list of frequently used verbs.
Some past participles forms are irregular and must be memorized.

INFINITIVE		AUXILIARY VERB	PAST PARTICIPLE
andare	to go	essere	
accendere	to turn on	avere	acceso
aprire	to open	avere	aperto
arrivare	to arrive	essere	
ballare	to dance	avere	
bere	to drink	avere	bevuto
cadere	to fall	essere	
camminare	to walk	avere	
cantare	to sing	avere	
chiedere	to ask	avere	chiesto
chiudere	to close	avere	chiuso
correggere	to correct	avere	corretto
decidere	to decide	avere	deciso
dipingere	to paint	avere	dipinto
dire	to say-to tell	avere	detto
diventare	to become	essere	
dormire	to sleep	avere	
entrare	to enter	essere	
essere	to be	essere	stato
fare	to do-to make	avere	fatto
giocare	to play	avere	
guardare	to look at-to watch	avere	
leggere	to read	avere	letto
mangiare	to eat	avere	
mettere	to put	avere	messo
morire	to die	essere	morto
nascere	to be born	essere	nato
nevicare	to snow	essere or avere	
offrire	to offer	avere	offerto
parlare	to speak	avere	
partire	to leave	essere	
perdere	to lose-to miss	avere	perduto-perso
piacere	to like	essere	piaciuto
piovere	to rain	essere or avere	piovuto
preferire	to prefer	avere	
prendere	to take	avere	preso
pulire	to clean	avere	
rimanere	to remain-to stay	essere	rimasto
rispondere	to answer	avere	risposto
ritornare	to return	essere	
rompere	to break	avere	rotto
salire	to get in	essere	
scegliere	to choose	avere	scelto
scendere	to get off	essere	sceso
scrivere	to write	avere	scritto
sentire	to hear-to tell	avere	
spegnere	to turn off	avere	spento
stare	to stay	essere	
studiare	to study	avere	
succedere	to happen	essere	successo
uscire	to go out-to leave	essere	
vedere	to see	avere	visto-veduto
venire	to come	essere	venuto
viaggiare	to travel	avere	

AGGETTIVI E PRONOMI POSSESSIVI, pp. 101-105

In Italian the possessive adjective refers to the possessor and must agree in gender and number with the person(s) or item(s) possessed.
The definite article must always be put in front of the possessive adjective

Italian forms of adjectives do not distinguish between il suo/i suoi (belonging to him) and la sua/le sue (belonging to her). What matters is the gender of the item possessed.

Nella camera di Carla c'è il suo (her-Carla's) cappotto
Nella camera di Carla ci sono i suoi (her-Carla's) pantaloni
Nella camera di Marco c'è la sua (his-Marco's) giacca
Nella camera di Marco ci sono le sue (his-Marco's) camicie

The adjective loro (*their*) is invariable.

Nella camera di Michele e Adriano	c'è	il loro (their-Michele and Adriano's) armadio
		la loro (their-Michele and Adriano's) scrivania
	ci sono	i loro (their-Michele and Adriano's) vestiti
		le loro (their-Michele and Adriano's) camicie

> **NOTE** *Whose is it? and whose are they? are expressed in Italian as: di chi è...?/ di chi sono...? (see p. 92).*
>
> ■ *Di chi è questo maglione?*   ■ *Whose sweater is this?*
> ● *È (il) mio*   ● *It's mine*
> ■ *Di chi sono le calze?*   ■ *Whose socks are these?*
> ● *Le calze sono di Adriano*   ● *They are Adriano's*
>
> *As you may notice another way to express possession is: di + the name of the possessor (le calze sono di Adriano).*

PRONOMI POSSESSIVI, pp. 94-105

Like the possessive adjective, the possessive pronoun must agree in gender and number with the noun it replaces. The forms of the possessive pronouns are identical to the forms of the possessive adjectives, and they are used *with* or *without* the definite article.

■ Di chi è questo cappotto?   ■ Whose coat is this?
● È (il) mio   ● It's mine
■ Di chi è questa giacca?   ■ Whose jacket is this?
● È (la) mia   ● It's mine
■ Di chi sono questi guanti?   ■ Whose gloves are these?
● Sono (i) miei   ● They are mine
■ Di chi sono queste camicie?   ■ Whose shirts are these?
● Sono (le) mie   ● They are mine

AGGETTIVI POSSESSIVI CON NOMI DI FAMIGLIA, pp. 101-105

The possessive adjective is used **without the article when referring to relatives in the singular**.
Loro always retains the article, as do possessive adjectives that refer to relatives in the plural.

mio zio (my uncle)	**i miei** zii
tuo cugino (your cousin)	**i tuoi** cugini
sua sorella (his/her sister)	**le sue** sorelle
nostra cugina (our female cousin)	**le nostre** cugine
vostra madre (your mother)	**le vostre** madri
il loro fratello (their brother)	**i loro** fratelli
la loro zia (their aunt)	**le loro** zie

If the noun expressing a family relationship is modified by an adjective or a suffix, the article is retained.
Papà, *mamma*, retain the article because they are considered terms of endearment.

È italiano **il tuo** papà? E **la tua** mamma?   Is your Dad Italian? And your Mum?

> **NOTE** *The possessive adjectives may follow the nouns to which they refer in order to emphasize the possession.*
>
> *Vieni a casa nostra?*   *Will you come to our house tonight?*
> *In camera tua ci sono due letti.*   *In your bedroom there are two beds.*
>
> *And in some expressions.*
>
> *Mamma mia!*
> *Dio mio!*

AGGETTIVO DIMOSTRATIVO *QUELLO*

The demonstrative adjective **quello** (*that/those*) has four forms which follow the pattern of the definite article. It precedes the noun it modifies.

Quel libro è italiano	**Quei** libri sono italiani
That book is Italian	Those books are Italian
Quello studente è gentile	**Quegli** studenti sono gentili
That student is nice	Those students are nice
Quell'orologio è d'oro	**Quegli** orologi sono d'oro
That watch is gold	Those watches are gold
Quella ragazza è simpatica	**Quelle** ragazze sono simpatiche
That girl is nice	Those girls are nice
Quell'aula è piccola	**Quelle** aule sono piccole
That classroom is small	Those classrooms are small

> **NOTE** *The adjective* **bello** *(handsome-beautiful-nice) usually precedes the noun and follows the pattern of the demonstrative adjective* **quello**.

	Maschile			Femminile	
Singolare		**Plurale**	**Singolare**		**Plurale**
quel		quei	quella/quell'		quelle
quello/quell'		quegli			
			bella/bell'		belle
bel		bei			
bello/bell'		begli			

AGGETTIVI NUMERALI ORDINALI, pp. 104-105

The aggettivi numerali ordinali (*ordinal numbers*) correspond to the English *first, second...* etc. In Italian they are used as regular adjectives and they have the four forms:

> primo, prima, primi, prime   (first)

After *decimo* (*tenth*) they are formed by dropping the final vowel of the corresponding cardinal number and adding -esimo:

> undici ➟ undicesimo   (eleventh)

Usually they precede the noun to which they refer and agree with it in gender and number.

■ Dove abita Stefano?　　　　　　　■ Where does Stefano live?
● Abita al sesto piano.　　　　　　　● On the sixth floor.

NOTE *The aggettivi numerali ordinali always follow proper names.*

■ *Non ricordo il nome del Papa attuale...*　　■ *I can't remember the name...*
● *Si chiama Giovanni Paolo secondo*　　　　● *His name is John Paul the second*

As for dates only the ordinal number il primo (the first) is used. Whereas the other dates are cardinal numbers.

■ *Che giorno è oggi?*　　　　　　　■ *What's the date today?*
● *Oggi è il primo novembre.*　　　　● *It's November, 1st.*

■ *E domani?*　　　　　　　　　　　■ *And tomorrow?*
● *È il due novembre.*　　　　　　　● *It's November, 2nd.*

FUTURO SEMPLICE, pp. 115-123

In Italian as in English the future tense is used to indicate an action which will take place at a future time.

In Italian the future is a simple tense, you do not need an auxiliary as in English (*will-shall*). To form the regular **futuro semplice** add to the stem of the verbs the appropriate endings (see pp. 115-123).

As in the present tense, verbs of the first conjugation ending in **-ciare** and **-giare** drop the **-i-** before adding the endings of the future to keep the soft sound of *-c-* and *-g-* (see p. 123).

cominciare	comincerò	I'll begin
mangiare	mangerò	I'll eat

Whereas verbs ending in **-care** and **-gare** add an **-h-** before the ending of the future to keep the hard sound of *-c-* and *-g-*.

cercare	cercherò	I'll look for
pagare	pagherò	I'll pay

There are also irregular verbs such as you can see on p. 124.

andare	to go	andrò, andrai, andrà, andremo, andrete, andranno
avere	to have	avrò, avrai, avrà, avremo, avrete, avranno
dovere	to have to-must	dovrò, dovrai, dovrà, dovremo, dovrete, dovranno
potere	can-may	potrò, potrai, potrà, potremo, potrete, potranno
sapere	to know	saprò, saprai, saprà, sapremo, saprete, sapranno
vedere	to see	vedrò, vedrai, vedrà, vedremo, vedrete, vedranno
bere	to drink	berrò, berrai, berrà, berremo, berrete, berranno
rimanere	to remain-to stay	rimarrò, rimarrai, rimarrà, rimarremo, rimarrete, rimarranno
tenere	to keep	terrò, terrai, terrà, terremo, terrete, terranno
tradurre	to translate	tradurrò, tradurrai, tradurrà, tradurremo, tradurrete, tradurranno
venire	to come	verrò, verrai, verrà, verremo, verrete, verranno
volere	to want	vorrò, vorrai, vorrà, vorremo, vorrete, vorranno
dare	to give	darò, darai, darà, daremo, darete, daranno
dire	to say-to tell	dirò, dirai, dirà, diremo, direte, diranno
essere	to be	sarò, sarai, sarà, saremo, sarete, saranno
fare	to do-to make	farò, farai, farà, faremo, farete, faranno
stare	to stay	starò, starai, starà, staremo, starete, staranno

In Italian the future tense is used also to make promises, to forecast events, to make plans (see pp. 119-120):

> **FARE PROMESSE**   (making promises)

Domani **smetterò** di fumare. Prometto!
Tomorrow I'll quit smoking. I promise!

> **FARE PREVISIONI**   (forecasting)

Secondo me, domani **tornerà** il bel tempo!
I think that tomorrow the weather will be nice again!

> **FARE PROGETTI**   (making plans)

L'anno prossimo **farò** un viaggio negli Stati Uniti!
Next year I'll travel to the States!

NOTE *In the common use of the language the future is usually expressed by the present tense + a future time expression.*

Domani vado a Venezia   *Tomorrow I'll go to Venice*

NOTE *In Italian the future can be used to express a probable fact, something that the person speaking feels is probably true. This is called the future of probability (see U 9, pp. 194-195; U 16, p. 344).*

■ *Che ore sono?*   ■ *What time is it?*
● *Non so, saranno le dieci*   ● *I don't know, it's probably ten o'clock*

FUTURO COMPOSTO, pp. 121-124

The **futuro composto** (*future perfect*) is used to express an action that will take place before another one in the future. As in English it is a compound tense formed by **the future of the verbs** *avere* or *essere* + **the past participle of the main verb**. With **essere** remember to agree the past participle in gender and number with the subject (see p. 121).

■ Quando tornerai nel tuo paese?   ■ When will you return to your country?
● Ci tornerò dopo che **avrò dato**   ● I'll return after I have taken
    l'esame di italiano   the Italian exam

PREPOSIZIONI ARTICOLATE, p. 124

In Italian there are eight prepositions: **di-a-da-in-con-su-per-tra** (or **fra**), these are the **preposizioni semplici**. As you can see in the box of page 124 the prepositions **di-a-da-in-su** combine with the definite article (when it is used) of the following noun and form contractions, they are called **preposizioni articolate.**

With the preposition con you can have a contraction or not, both forms are correct. The prepositions per and tra (or fra) do not combine with the article and you must have two separate words.

> NOTE *The preposizioni semplici are invariable, they do not agree in gender and number.*

SAPERE E CONOSCERE, p. 110

Sapere and conoscere both translate as *to know* but they are not interchangeable. Conoscere is *to know* in the sense of *to be acquainted with, to meet, to make the acquaintance of.* Conoscere is always followed by a noun (usually a geographical site or a person).

Conosco Francesco/Venezia   I know Francesco/Venice

Sapere is *to know a fact, to have knowledge of.*

So il numero di telefono di Mauro   I know Mauro's telephone number
So quando parte il treno per Firenze   I know when the train to Florence will leave

Sapere also means *to know how, can,* and in this case expresses capability and it is followed by an infinitive.

So cucinare   I can cook/I know how to cook

Equivalent expressions are: sono capace di + infinitive verb and sono bravo/a a (in) + infinitive verb.

Non sono capace di riparare la TV   I can't repair TV (I'm incapable of repairing TV)
Sono bravo/a a lavorare a maglia   I can knit (I'm good at knitting)

VERBI RIFLESSIVI, pp. 132-133

The verbi riflessivi (*reflexive verbs*) are called reflexive because they reflect their actions on the subject. They are conjugated regularly but they are preceded by reflexive pronouns which will change according to the subjects.

Reflexive pronouns are placed before a conjugated verb or attached to the infinitive (which drops the final -*e*) (see pp. 132-133).

(io) Mi sveglio presto	I wake (myself) up early
Ho l'abitudine di svegliarmi presto	I am used to waking up early

If the infinitive is preceded by a form of dovere, potere, or volere, the reflexive pronoun is either attached to the infinitive or placed before the conjugated verb.

Voglio svegliarmi presto	
or Mi voglio svegliare presto	I want to wake up early

Many transitive verbs (verbs that take a direct object) can be made reflexive such as the examples on p. 130.

Alfredo lava la sua macchina	Alfredo is washing his car
La mattina Alfredo si lava	Alfredo washes himself every day

Italian uses reflexive constructions more frequently than English.
The English expressions *to get* and *to become* are often rendered in Italian with a reflexive construction.

Maria si pettina	Mary combs her hair
Alberto si veste e esce	Alberto gets dressed and leaves

NOTE *Here is a list of the most common reflexive verbs:*

accorgersi/rendersi conto di	*to realize*
addormentarsi	*to fall asleep*
alzarsi	*to get up*
annoiarsi	*to get bored*
arrabbiarsi	*to get angry*
asciugarsi	*to dry oneself*
bagnarsi	*to get wet*
divertirsi	*to have fun*
farsi la barba	*to shave*
fidanzarsi	*to get engaged*
guardarsi	*to look at oneself*
innamorarsi (di)	*to fall in love (with)*
lamentarsi	*to complain*
laurearsi	*to graduate*
lavarsi	*to wash up*
mettersi	*to put on*

>

pettinarsi	to comb one's hair
riposarsi	to rest
sentirsi	to feel oneself
spazzolarsi	to brush one's hair
specializzarsi	to specialize
spogliarsi	to get undressed
sposarsi	to get married
stancarsi	to get tired
svegliarsi	to wake up
tagliarsi	to cut oneself
togliersi	to take off
trovarsi	to find oneself-to get along
truccarsi	to put on make up
vergognarsi	to be embarassed
vestirsi	to get dressed

VERBI RECIPROCI, p. 131

The reflexive construction with the three plural reflexive pronouns **ci**, **vi**, **si** is also used to express reciprocal action (*each other*).

Arturo e Elide **si baciano**   Arturo and Elide are kissing (each other)

NOTE *Alcuni verbi reciproci:*

aiutarsi	to help each other
amarsi	to love each other
baciarsi	to kiss each other
conoscersi	to get to know
darsi un appuntamento	to make an appointment
guardarsi	to look at each other
incontrarsi	to meet each other
lasciarsi	to split up
odiarsi	to hate each other
salutarsi	to greet each other
scriversi	to write to each other
telefonarsi	to call each other

PASSATO PROSSIMO DEI VERBI RIFLESSIVI, pp. 133-148

The **passato prossimo** of reflexive verbs is always formed with the present tense of the auxiliary *essere* + the past participle which agrees with the subject in gender and number.

(io) **Mi sono** addormentato/a alle dieci   I fell asleep at ten o'clock
(noi) **Ci siamo** addormentati/e alle dieci   We fell asleep at ten o'clock

IMPERFETTO, pp. 168-177-178-179

The **imperfetto** (*imperfect*) is the form of a verb used to show incomplete action in the past. Whereas the *passato prossimo* expresses a completed action in the past.
In Italian the *imperfetto* is a simple tense.

The **imperfetto** is formed by adding the appropriate endings to the stem of the verb (see p. 168).

Some verbs have irregular forms.

bere	(to drink)	bevevo, bevevi, beveva, bevevamo, bevevate, bevevano
dire	(to say-to tell)	dicevo, dicevi, diceva, dicevamo, dicevate, dicevano
essere	(to be)	ero, eri, era, eravamo, eravate, erano
fare	(to do-to make)	facevo, facevi, faceva, facevamo, facevate, facevano
tradurre	(to translate)	traducevo, traducevi, traduceva, traducevamo, traducevate, traducevano

---

The **imperfetto** is used to express (see pp. 178-179):

1. **Azioni passate contemporanee** (past contemporary actions)

~~~~~~~~   **imperfetto + imperfetto**

Contemporary actions in progress in the past, often expressed in English with the past progressive.

Mentre **mangiavo, guardavo** la TV   While I was eating I was watching TV
Leggevo e ascoltavo la musica   I was reading and listening to music

2. **Azione passata interrotta da un'altra** (past action interrupted by another)

--~~\/~--   **imperfetto + passato prossimo**
          passato prossimo + imperfetto

The *imperfetto* conveys an ongoing event, a state already in progress (doing something, reading, eating) or a description of a state interrupted by another event that occurred at a specific moment (*passato prossimo*: arrival, a telephone call).

Mentre **mangiavo, ha suonato** il telefono   While I was eating the telephone rang
Quando **è arrivato** Gino, **studiavo**   When Gino arrived I was studying   >

19

3. Azioni passate ripetute per abitudine (past routines and habits)

∧∧∧   imperfetto

To describe repeated or recurrent actions in the past. The *imperfetto* is the tense of habit and routine. It tells what people used to do or things that used to happen.

The following time expressions frequently signal the use of the imperfect and indicate repetition of action in the past.

Di solito	usually
Ogni giorno	everyday
Tutti i giorni	every day
Da bambino	when I was a child
Quando ero bambino	when I was a child
Quando avevo ... anni	when I was ... years old

Durante le vacanze di solito dormivo molto   During my vacations I used to sleep a lot

Da ragazzo andavo al mare tutti i venerdì   When I was a boy I used to go to the seaside every Friday

4. Descrizione di persone, animali, situazioni, luoghi, ambienti (description of persons, animals, situations and places)

∿∿∿   imperfetto

To describe the outside world, animals and people, including physical and emotional states.

Mio nonno era un uomo molto simpatico   My grandfather was a very nice man

Quando sono andata al mare,   When I went to the seaside,
il cielo era sereno e il mare era calmo   the sky was clear and the sea was calm

Alla festa di Franco c'era molta   At Franco's party there were a lot of
gente simpatica   nice people

TRAPASSATO PROSSIMO, pp. 177-179

The trapassato prossimo is the equivalent of the English *past perfect (I had seen)*. It is used to express a completed action in the past that occurred before another past event. The other past event can be in the *passato prossimo*, in the *imperfetto*, or simply implied.
The *trapassato prossimo* is formed with the imperfect form of the auxiliary verbs *avere* or *essere* + *past participle* (with *essere* the *past participle* always agrees with the subject in gender and number).

Oggi in libreria è arrivato il libro   Today, the book I had ordered
che (io) avevo ordinato un mese fa   one month ago, arrived

Quando è cominciato a piovere   When it began raining,
(io) ero già tornata a casa da mezz'ora   I had already been back for half an hour

PRONOMI DIRETTI, pp. 188-189-190-200-202-203

Many verbs have a direct object noun, which is the answer to the questions *whom?* or *what?*
Direct object pronouns replace the direct object nouns.

Incontro Angelo e lo saluto	When I meet Angelo I say hello! (to him)
Incontro Carla e la saluto	When I meet Carla I say hello! (to her)

■ Bevi il caffè?   ■ Do you drink coffee?
● Sì lo bevo   ● Yes I drink it

Ho perso le chiavi. Le ho perse ieri	I lost the keys. I lost them yesterday

The names Angelo and Carla are direct object nouns. They are the answer to the question *whom?* The nouns coffee and keys answer to the question *what?*

Direct object pronouns are placed immediately before a conjugated verb (see p. 189).

Carlo, mi aspetti dopo la lezione?	Carlo, will you wait for me after class?

In a negative sentence, the word non must precede the object pronoun.

No, non ti aspetto	No, I won't wait for you

Lo and la are usually elided before the verb *avere* in the forms beginning with h or the verbs starting with a vowel. The plural forms li and le are never elided (see p. 200).

Ho incontrato Angelo e l'ho invitato	I met Angelo and I invited him
Ho incontrato Carla e l'ho invitata	I met Carla and I invited her
Ho incontrato Carlo e Alberto e li ho invitati	I met Carlo and Alberto and I invited them
Ho incontrato Stefania e Stella e le ho invitate	I met Stefania and Stella and I invited them

In the case of the singular formal *you*, the direct object pronoun La (capitalized) refers to both feminine and masculine.

Professor Mazzetti, La aspetto dopo la lezione	Professor Mazzetti, I'll wait for you after the lesson
Signora Rossi, La aspetto al bar	Mrs. Rossi, I'll wait for you at the bar

Li is used when masculine and feminine nouns appear together.

■ Conosci Angelo e Carla?   ■ Do you know Angelo and Carla?
● Sì, li conosco   ● Yes, I know them

> NOTE *If the infinitive is preceded by a form of* dovere, potere, volere, *the object pronoun may be either attached to the infinitive dropping the last* -e, *or placed before the conjugated verb (see p. 188).*
>
> *Ecco Angelo! Voglio invitarlo!*   Here is Angelo! I want to invite him
> *or Lo voglio invitare subito!*   I want to invite him immediately!

Lo also substitutes for entire subordinate clauses, and is never omitted in an answer involving the verb **sapere** (see p. 195).

- Sai che ore sono?
- Sì, **lo** so

- Do you know what time it is?
- Yes, I do

- Sa perché Gina non è venuta?
- No, non **lo** so

- Do you know why Gina didn't come?
- No, I don't

NE, pp. 190-202-203

Answering a question about quantity, Italian requires the use of **ne** to replace the direct object.
Ne is invariable and replaces masculine/feminine singular and plural objects.

- Quanti maglioni compri?
- **Ne** compro uno

- How many sweaters will you buy?
- I'll buy one (of them)

- Quante magliette compri?
- **Ne** compro molte

- How many T-shirts will you buy?
- I'll buy a lot (of them)

Uno-una (*one*), **alcuni-alcune** (*some*), **pochi-poche** (*few*), **molti-molte** (*many*), **nessuno-nessuna** (*any of them*) agree with the object.

- Quante magliette compri?
- **Ne** compro alcune

- How many T-shirts will you buy?
- I'll buy a few (of them)

Nessuno-nessuna can never be made plural and require **non** in front of the verb.

- Quante magliette compri?
- **Non ne** compro nessuna

- How many T-shirts will you buy?
- I won't buy any (of them)

In the combination **c'è/ci sono + ne** (*there is/there are*), **ci** in front of **ne** becomes **ce**.

- Quanti studenti ci sono nell'aula?
- **Ce n'è** uno
- **Ce ne** sono (dieci) molti

- How many students are in the classroom?
- There is one (of them)
- There are (ten) many

PRONOMI DIRETTI E PASSATO PROSSIMO, pp. 200-202-203

When you have the direct object pronouns **lo**, **la**, **li**, **le**, and **ne** and a compound tense formed with the auxiliary verb *avere*, **the past participle** must **agree in gender and number** with the direct object pronouns.

The pronouns **lo-la** in front of **h** and **vowels** usually elide -o and -a and add an apostrophe, but not **li-le**

Ho incontrato il professore, **l'ho** invitato alla festa	I met the professor, I invited him to the party
Ho incontrato la mia amica, **l'ho** invitata alla festa	I met my friend, I invited her to the party
Ho incontrato i miei colleghi, **li ho** invitati alla festa	I met my collegues, I invited them to the party
Ho incontrato le mie amiche, **le ho** invitate alla festa	I met my friends, I invited them to the party

■ Quanti libri hai comprato?
● **Ne** ho comprati molti

■ How many books did you buy?
● I bought a lot (of them)

■ Quante riviste hai comprato?
● **Ne** ho comprata una

■ How many magazines did you buy?
● I bought one (of them)

PRONOMI INDIRETTI, pp. 212-223

Indirect object pronouns replace indirect object nouns. In Italian they answer the question *a chi?*

> **NOTE** *In English the preposition to (to whom?) is not always required.*

- ■ **A chi** scrivi?
- ● Scrivo **a Piero**. **Gli** scrivo tutti i giorni

- ■ To whom are you writing?
- ● I'm writing to Piero. I write (to) him every day

Indirect object pronouns are identical in form to direct object pronouns, except for the third person singular **gli-le** and plural **gli**. They precede, like direct object pronouns, a conjugated verb and **they do not agree in gender and number with the past participle**. The third singular forms **le-gli** never elide in front of verbs beginning with *h-* or *vowel* (see p. 223).

Giorgio **mi** ha dato un passaggio al centro	Giorgio gave me a lift to the centre
Giorgio **ti** ha prestato il suo dizionario	Giorgio lent his dictionary to you
Giorgio **ci** ha venduto la sua macchina	Giorgio sold his car to us
Giorgio **vi** ha chiesto un favore	Giorgio asked you (plural) a favour
Giorgio **gli** ha regalato un orologio	Giorgio gave him a watch
Giorgio **le** ha scritto una cartolina da Parigi	Giorgio wrote a postcard to her from Paris
Giorgio **gli** ha prestato il suo dizionario	Giorgio lent his dictionary to them

The indirect pronoun **Le** (capitalized) is formal (referring to masculine and feminine singular).

Professore, Giorgio **Le** ha promesso di tornare presto?	Professor, did Giorgio promise you (formal) he would return soon?
Signora, Giorgio **Le** ha promesso di tornare presto?	Madam, did Giorgio promise you (formal) he would return soon?

> **NOTE** *Indirect object pronouns are attached to an infinitive, and the -e of the infinitive is dropped.*
>
> *Non è possibile parlargli*   *It's not possible to talk to him*
> *Ho voglia di scriverle*   *I feel like writing to her*
>
> *If the infinitive is preceded by a form of dovere, potere, volere, the indirect object pronoun is either attached to the infinitive dropping -e or placed before the conjugated verb.*
>
> *Voglio parlargli*   or   *Gli voglio parlare*   *I want to talk to him*

PIACERE, pp. 212-216

Piacere expresses *to like* and it is more similar to the English phrase to be pleasing to.

A Gianni piace la musica popolare	Gianni likes folk music (folk music is pleasing to him)
A Maria piacciono le canzoni popolari	Maria likes folk songs (folk songs are pleasing to her)

A Gianni and a Maria correspond to the English subject (*Gianni, Maria*) and the English objects *folk music, folk songs* i.e. the things that are liked, are the subjects of the sentences. It means that you have to conjugate piacere with the thing(s) liked. Therefore you use primarily two forms of *piacere: piace/piacciono*. *Piacere* requires the indirect object pronouns.

Gli (or a Gianni) piace la musica popolare
Le (or a Maria) piacciono le canzoni popolari

Mi piace questo pittore	I like this painter (this painter is pleasing to me)
Ci piacciono i dipinti di Tiziano	We like Tiziano's paintings (Tiziano's paintings are pleasing to us)

> NOTE *When the indirect object is a noun, it must be preceded by the preposition a:*
>
> *a Gianni, a Maria, ai miei amici, agli studenti...*

When the subject of *piacere* is a verb or a series of verbs, *piacere* is conjugated in the third person singular and followed by the infinitive of the verb(s) (see p. 212).

Ti piace visitare i musei	You like visiting museums
Le piace giocare a tennis	She likes playing tennis

> NOTE *Dispiacere means* to be sorry *and it is used in the same way as* piacere *(see p. 216).*
>
> *Mi dispiace (di) partire* — *I am sorry to leave*
> *Gli è dispiaciuto rimanere solo* — *He was sorry to be left alone*
>
> To dislike *is expressed with the negative of* piacere. *Observe the word order in negative senteces:*
> *Non vi piace la pizza Margherita* — *You don't like pizza Margherita*

Piacere is conjugated with essere in compound tenses, therefore its past participle agrees in gender and number with the subject (the things liked) (see p. 216).

Ti è piaciuto il libro?	Did you like the book?
Le sono piaciuti i protagonisti del film?	Did you (formal) like the characters in the movie?

25

The following verbs are used with the indirect object nouns and pronouns as *piacere*:

bastare to be enough

Non **mi basta** il tempo	I don't have enough time
Mi bastano i soldi	I have enough money
Non **mi sono bastati** i soldi	I did not have enough money

mancare to miss

Mi manca Francesco	I miss Francesco
Mi mancano i miei genitori	I miss my parents

In time clauses *mancare* is used without the indirect object pronouns.

Manca un mese alla partenza per le vacanze	Another month before the holidays start
Mancano tre settimane alla partenza per le vacanze	Another three weeks before the holidays start

servire to need-to be necessary

Mi serve un amico	I need a friend
Mi servono molti soldi	I need a lot of money

interessare to be interested in to be important for/to care

Al professore **interessa** la politica, **gli** interessa molto	Professor is interested in politics, he is very interested in it
Queste cose non **interessano** a Daniela, non **le** interessano affatto	These things are not important for Daniela, she doesn't care

PRONOMI INDIRETTI - FORMA TONICA, p. 223

In addition to the forms studied before, the indirect object pronouns have other forms called *forma tonica*: **a me** (*to me*), **a te** (*to you* sing.), **a lui** (*to him*) **a lei** (*to her*), **a noi** (*to us*), **a voi** (*to you* plural), **a loro** (*to them* mascul. and femin.).

These pronouns are used when a special emphasis on the indirect object pronoun must be expressed. **They can be preceded by all prepositions**

■ A chi scrivi la lettera?	■ Whom are you writing the letter to?
● La scrivo **a te**	● I'm writing it to you
■ A chi dai il tuo indirizzo?	■ Whom are you giving your address to?
● Lo do **a lui**	● I'm giving it to him
■ Maria, esci **con me**?	■ Maria, will you go out with me?
● No grazie, non posso	● No, thanks, I can't
■ Per chi è questo libro?	■ For whom is this book?
● Questo libro è **per lei**	● This book is for her
■ Vieni **con noi** al cinema?	■ Will you come with us to the movie?
● Sì, vengo con voi	● Yes, I'll come with you

CONDIZIONALE SEMPLICE, p. 229

The **condizionale semplice** (*present conditional*) is a simple tense, you do not need an auxiliary verb like in English (*would-should*). To form the present conditional add to the stem of the verb the appropriate endings (see p. 229).

Verbs ending in -care and -gare add an -h- between the stem and the endings to keep the hard sound of -*c*- and -*g*- (see p. 247).

cercare	cercherei	I would look for
pagare	pagherei	I would pay

Verbs ending in -ciare and -giare drop the -i- before the endings of the conditional to keep the soft sound of -*c*- and -*g*-.

cominciare	comincerei	I would begin
mangiare	mangerei	I would eat

NOTE *There are irregular verbs such as you can see on p. 247.*

andare	*andrei, andresti, andrebbe, andremmo, andreste, andrebbero*
avere	*avrei, avresti, avrebbe, avremmo, avreste, avrebbero*
bere	*berrei, berresti, berrebbe, berremmo, berreste, berrebbero*
dare	*darei, daresti, darebbe, daremmo, dareste, darebbero*
dire	*direi, diresti, direbbe, diremmo, direste, direbbero*
dovere	*dovrei, dovresti, dovrebbe, dovremmo, dovreste, dovrebbero*
essere	*sarei, saresti, sarebbe, saremmo, sareste, sarebbero*
fare	*farei, faresti, farebbe, faremmo, fareste, farebbero*
potere	*potrei, potresti, potrebbe, potremmo, potreste, potrebbero*
rimanere	*rimarrei, rimarresti, rimarrebbe, rimarremmo, rimarreste, rimarrebbero*
sapere	*saprei, sapresti, saprebbe, sapremmo, sapreste, saprebbero*
stare	*starei, staresti, starebbe, staremmo, stareste, starebbero*
tenere	*terrei, terresti, terrebbe, terremmo, terreste, terrebbero*
tradurre	*tradurrei, tradurresti, tradurrebbe, tradurremmo, tradurreste, tradurrebbero*
vedere	*vedrei, vedresti, vedrebbe, vedremmo, vedreste, vedrebbero*
venire	*verrei, verresti, verrebbe, verremmo, verreste, verrebbero*
volere	*vorrei, vorresti, vorrebbe, vorremmo, vorreste, vorrebbero*

In Italian the conditional is mainly used to express wishes, to formulate polite requests and to give advice. The conditional is also used to report hearsay or unsubstantiated news in the journalistic style (see p. 246).

ESPRIMERE UN DESIDERIO (a wish)

- Con questo caldo berrei volentieri una birra!
- Anch'io avrei voglia di qualcosa di fresco!

- It's hot, I would like to drink a beer !
- Me too, I would like something cold!

CHIEDERE QUALCOSA IN MODO GENTILE (polite request)

Scusa Simone, ti dispiacerebbe prestarmi dei soldi? Ho lasciato il portafoglio a casa!

Simone, would you mind lending me some money? I left my wallet at home!

DARE CONSIGLI (giving advice)

- Vorrei cambiare tipo di studi, che ne pensi?
- Io ci penserei bene prima di cambiare

- I would like to change the subject I am studying, what do you think about it?
- I would think twice before changing

CONDIZIONALE COMPOSTO, pp. 236-247

The condizionale composto (*conditional perfect*) is a compound tense and is formed by the condizionale semplice of the verbs *avere* or *essere* + the past participle of the main verb. With essere remember to agree the past participle with the subject in gender and number. It is used, as in English, in a sequence of tenses in the past.

Ieri avrei fatto una passeggiata, ma pioveva

Yesterday I would have walked, but it was raining

La settimana scorsa Anna sarebbe andata a Firenze, ma ha dovuto lavorare

Last week Anna would have gone to Florence, but she had to work

COMPARATIVI E SUPERLATIVI, pp. 256-268

The comparativo indicates a greater degree (superiority), a lesser degree (inferiority), or an equal degree (equality) of the quality, expressed by an adjective, of a person or thing compared with another (see p. 256). The comparativo di maggioranza (*comparative of superiority*) is formed by:

> più + the adjective + di (with or without articles) or che

Paolo è più alto di Antonio	Paolo is taller than Antonio
L'aereo è più veloce del treno	The plane is faster than the train

The comparativo di minoranza (*comparative of inferiority*) is formed by:

> meno + the adjective + di (with or without articles) or che

Antonio è meno alto di Paolo	Antonio is shorter than Paolo
Il treno è meno veloce dell'aereo	The train is slower than the plane

The comparativo di uguaglianza (*comparative of equality*) is formed by:

> (così) + the adjective + come
> or
> (tanto) + the adjective + quanto

Antonio è (così) simpatico come Paolo	Antonio is as nice as Paolo
L'autobus è (tanto) comodo quanto il treno	The bus is as comfortable as the train

> **NOTE** *Usually* così *and* tanto *are omitted.*

The conjunction che is used instead of di when the comparison (of superiority or inferiority) refers to the same subject, and it is between two adjectives, two nouns, two verbs in the infinitive form, or two nouns preceded by a preposition.

Questa torta è più bella che buona	This cake looks better than it tastes
Gli italiani bevono più vino che birra	Italians drink more wine than beer
Maria viaggia più volentieri in macchina che in treno	Mary prefers travelling by car than by train

> **NOTE** *Before a conjugated verb* than *is expressed by* di quello che.
>
> *Questo libro è* **più** *interessante* **di quello che** *credevo*   *This book is more interesting than I thought*

ALTRE FORME DI COMPARATIVI, p. 268

The adjectives **buono** (*good*), **cattivo** (*bad*), **grande** (*big*), **piccolo** (*small*), have two forms for the comparison of superiority.

buono	⇒	**migliore**	or	più buono	better		
cattivo	⇒	**peggiore**	or	più cattivo	worse		
grande	⇒	**maggiore**	or	più grande	bigger	or	older
piccolo	⇒	**minore**	or	più piccolo	smaller	or	younger

> **NOTE** *The adverbs* **bene** (*well*) *and* **male** (*badly*) *qualify a verb and their forms of comparison of superiority are* **meglio** *and* **peggio**
>
> *Oggi sto* **meglio**   *Today I feel better*
>
> *Ieri stavo* **peggio**   *Yesterday I felt worse*

SUPERLATIVO ASSOLUTO, p. 268

The **superlativo assoluto** (*absolute superlative*) is used to intensify the quality expressed by the adjective (or adverb) implying no comparison. It is formed by:

a) dropping the final vowel of the masculine plural form of the adjective (or dropping the final vowel of the adverb) and adding the suffix **-issimo/a** for the singular adjectives and **-issimi/e** for the plural adjectives.

Mio zio è **ricchissimo**	My uncle is very rich
Sono tornato a casa **tardissimo**	I returned home very late

b) using **molto** or **tanto** (invariable) in front of the adjective or the adverb.

Mio zio è **tanto ricco**	My uncle is very rich
Sono tornato a casa **molto tardi**	I returned home very late

c) combining adjectives to emphasize the quality:

Mio zio è **ricco sfondato**	My uncle is rolling in money

ALTRE FORME DI SUPERLATIVI ASSOLUTI, p. 268

The following adjectives have two forms for the absolute superlative.

buono	➡	**ottimo**	or	buonissimo	very good
cattivo	➡	**pessimo**	or	cattivissimo	very bad
grande	➡	**massimo**	or	grandissimo	very big
piccolo	➡	**minimo**	or	piccolissimo	very small

SUPERLATIVO RELATIVO, p. 259

The **superlativo relativo** (*relative superlative*) expresses the highest degree of a quality (adjective/adverb) with reference to more than one other person or thing of the same class. The relative superlatives of superiority or inferiority are formed by:

> **the definite article + the comparative form + *di* or *in***

La Ferrari è l'automobile **più** famosa **del** mondo   Ferrari is the most famous car in the world

Il calcio è **lo** sport **più** popolare d'Italia   Soccer is the most popular sport in Italy

ALTRE FORME DI SUPERLATIVI RELATIVI, p. 268

The following adjectives have two forms for the relative superlatives.

buono	➡	**il migliore**	or	il più buono	the best		
cattivo	➡	**il peggiore**	or	il più cattivo	the worst		
grande	➡	**il maggiore**	or	il più grande	the biggest	or	the oldest
piccolo	➡	**il minore**	or	il più piccolo	the smallest	or	the youngest

PRONOMI COMBINATI, pp. 265-269

A verb can have, in the same sentence, a direct and an indirect object pronoun: **pronome combinato** When this is the case both pronouns precede the verb and the indirect object pronoun is before the direct object pronoun.
The indirect object pronouns **mi-ti-ci-vi** turn the final *-i* into *-e* before the direct object pronouns **lo-la-li-le** and before **ne**

■ Mi presti la macchina? **Me la** presti
    fino a domani?
● Sì **te la** presto

■ Can you lend me your car? Can you lend it
    to me until tomorrow?
● Yes I'll lend it to you

■ Quante cassette ti presta Maria?
● Me ne presta due

■ How many cassettes is Mary lending to you?
● She is lending me two (of them)

The indirect pronouns gli and le turn into glie... and combine with the direct object pronouns lo-la-li-le to form one word.

Le presto il mio motorino,
glielo presto subito

I'll lend my moped to her,
I'll lend it to her now

Anna gli presta la sua macchina,
gliela presta volentieri

Anna is lending her car to him,
she is happy to lend it to him

When the verb is a compound tense, the past participle agrees in number and gender with the *direct object pronouns* and *ne* (see p. 266).

Aldo mi ha portato un regalo,
me l'ha portato per il mio compleanno

Aldo brought me a gift,
he brought it to me for my birthday

Aldo mi ha portato dei fiori,
me li ha portati per il mio compleanno

Aldo brought me some flowers,
he brought them to me for my birthday

■ Quanti regali ti ha fatto Paolo?
● Me ne ha fatti moltissimi

■ How many gifts did you receive from Paolo?
● A lot (of them)

With the verbs potere-dovere-volere the combined pronouns can stand in front of the verbs or attached to the infinitive dropping the last *-e*.

Se vuoi il dizionario, te lo posso prestare io
or Se vuoi il dizionario, posso prestartelo io

If you want the dictionary, I can lend it to you

When in the sentence there is an infinitive, the combined pronouns must be attached to the end dropping the last *-e*.

Ho bisogno di dirti una cosa,
ho bisogno di dirtela subito!

I must tell you something now!

IMPERATIVO, pp. 281-291-296-297

The imperativo (*imperative*) is the command form of the verb and is used to give orders, directions, instructions, advice, permission (see pp. 296-297).

DARE ORDINI (giving orders)

- ■ Paolo, va subito in camera tua e studia!
- ● D'accordo, mamma!

- ■ Paolo, go to your room and study!
- ● Okay, Mum!

DARE INDICAZIONI (giving directions)

- ■ Scusi, dov'è la Banca Nazionale?
- ● Prenda la prima strada a sinistra e poi vada diritto…

- ■ Excuse me, where is the National Bank?
- ● Take the first street on the left and then go straight on…

DARE ISTRUZIONI (giving instructions)

- ■ Mi scusi, che devo fare per telefonare in Germania?
- ● Faccia il prefisso 0049, poi il prefisso della città…

- ■ Excuse me, what should I dial to call Germany?
- ● Dial 0049 for Germany, then the area code…

DARE CONSIGLI (giving advice)

- ■ Non so come fare a convincere Laura ad uscire con me…
- ● Sii molto gentile, telefonale spesso e mandale subito un mazzo di fiori!

- ■ I don't know how to convince Laura to come out with me…
- ● Be very kind, call her often and send her a bunch of flowers!

DARE UN PERMESSO (giving permission)

- ■ Permette una parola, Signora Bianchi?
- ● Prego, dica pure!

- ■ Can I ask you something, Mrs. Bianchi?
- ● Certainly!

To form the imperative add to the stem of the verb the appropriate endings (see p. 281).
The verbs **essere** and **avere** have irregular imperative forms (see p. 281).

> NOTE *The first plural imperative form (noi) corresponds to the English let's + infinitive.*
> *The third plural imperative form (Loro) which is the formal plural, is not commonly used. To address*
> *more than one person the second plural form (voi) is commonly used.*

The **imperativo negativo** (*negative imperative*) is formed by placing **non + the imperative forms** except
for the second singular form (*tu*) which is made up of **non + infinitive** (see p. 281).

(voi) **Non** us**ate** il dizionario!	(you/plural) Don't use the dictionary!
(tu) **Non** fum**are**!	(you) Don't smoke!

When in a sentence the **imperative is followed by pronouns** (simple and combined forms) and **ne**, or by
the adverb **ci**, they are attached at the end of the verb for the *tu-noi-voi* forms **but they precede** the *Lei*
(formal singular *you*) and *Loro* (formal plural *you*) forms (see p. 291).

Giulio vorrebbe il giornale	(tu) compra**glielo**!	Giulio would like to have the newspaper	(you) buy it for him!	
	(voi) comprate**glielo**!		(you pl.) buy it for him!	
	(noi) compriamo**glielo**!		(we) let's buy it for him!	
	(Lei) **glielo** compri!		(you) buy it for him!	
	(Loro) **glielo** comprino!		(you pl.) buy it for him!	

When the verb is **imperativo negativo** (*negative imperative*) **the pronouns** may either precede or follow the
verb with *tu-noi-voi* forms. With *Lei* and *Loro* forms pronouns must be stand in front.

L'autobus è già arrivato	(tu) **non** perder**lo**! **non lo** perdere!	The bus has already arrived	(you) don't miss it!
	(noi) **non** perdiamo**lo**! **non lo** perdiamo!		(we) let's not miss it!
	(voi) **non** perdete**lo**! **non lo** perdete!		(you pl.) don't miss it!
	(Lei) **non lo** perda! (Loro) **non lo** perdano!		(you) don't miss it! (you pl.) don't miss it!

The verbs **dire-andare-fare-dare-stare** have irregular imperative forms (see pp. 296-297).
When the *tu* form of these verbs is followed by *pronouns* (simple or combined forms) and *ne* or by the adverb
ci, the first consonant of the pronoun is doubled except when the pronoun is *gli* (see pp. 293-294).

Se vuoi andare a casa, vacci!	If you want to go home, go (there)!
Stammi a sentire, devo raccontarti una cosa!	Listen to me, I must tell you somenthing!
La mia macchina non funziona, dammi la tua, dammela fino a stasera!	My car doesn't work, give me your car (could I borrow yours?), give it to me (may I borrow it?) till tonight!
Se vedi Paolo, digli di telefonarmi!	If you see Paolo, tell him to call me!

PRONOMI RELATIVI, pp. 307-313

The **pronome relativo** (*relative pronoun*) as a pronoun stands for a noun previously mentioned (the antecedent) and introduces a subordinate clause, a relative clause which gives additional information about the antecedent.
In Italian the relative pronouns must always be expressed.

When the relative pronoun is the **subject** or the **object** of the relative clause it is **che**, invariable and can be referred to persons or things (see p. 307).

Non conosco	il ragazzo la ragazza i ragazzi le ragazze	che	entra in questo momento entrano in questo momento hai salutato	I don't know	the boy the girl the boys the girls	that/who whom	is entering right now are entering right now you greeted

Il quale, **la quale**, **i quali**, **le quali** are relative pronouns of more formal usage which can be used as subject or object of the relative clause and must agree in gender and number with the noun to which they refer (see p. 313).

When the relative pronoun is preceded by prepositions it is **cui** (**invariable**) or **il quale**, **la quale**, **i quali**, **le quali** (they agree in gender and number with the noun to which they refer, and the articles combine with the prepositions **di**, **a**, **da**, **in**, **su**) (see p. 307).

Non conosco il ragazzo	a cui/ al quale	hai offerto un caffè	I dont' know the boy	for (to) whom	you bought a coffee

Non conosco la ragazza	di cui/ della quale	stai parlando	I dont' know the girl	about whom	you are speaking

Non conosco i ragazzi	per cui/ per i quali	vuoi comprare un regalo	I dont' know the boy's	for whom	you want to by a gift

Non conosco le ragazze	con cui/ con le quali	esci stasera	I dont' know the girls	with whom	you are going out tonight

The relative pronouns quello che/ciò che meaning *what* (*that which*) occur without an antecedent. They are invariable in form and can function as subject or object (see p. 307).

So bene quello che/ciò che faccio   I know what I am doing

Ho pensato a quello che/ciò che mi hai detto   I thought of what you said to me

---

NOTE *Chi (who) in Italian is an interrogative pronoun (*Chi *è? Who is it?).*

It can also be a relative pronoun which refers to persons. It corresponds to the English the one(s) who-he/she who. It is invariable and the verb following is always in the third person singular. It is mainly used in proverbs or to make generalizations.

Chi cerca trova!   *He/The one who looks, will find!*

Chi frequenta le lezioni impara   *Those/The ones who attend the lessons learn a lot*

CI, p. 310

Ci can be used as a pronoun:

– as a reflexive pronoun (*ourselves*):

La mattina ci alziamo presto   In the morning we get up early

– as a direct object pronoun (*us*):

Quando ci ha visto, il professore   When he saw us, the professor
ci ha invitato a prendere un caffè   invited us for a coffee

– as an indirect object pronoun (*to us*):

Giorgio ci ha telefonato e ci ha chiesto   When Giorgio telephoned (to) us, he asked (to) us
di accompagnarlo alla stazione   to take him to the station

Ci is used as an adverb with reference to a previously mentioned place or situation and is mainly introduced by the prepositions in, a, su, con even when not expressed but implicit.

Vado a Roma e ci resto due settimane   I'm going to Rome, I'll be staying there for two weeks

■ Chi compra il pane?   ■ Who is going to buy bread?
● Ci penso io (a comprare il pane)   ● I'll take care of it

Marco è molto simpatico: Marco is very nice,
ci (con lui) sto bene!   I like his company!

With the verbs vedere and sentire, ci reinforces the meaning.

Ci vedo poco con questi occhiali, perciò devo comprarne un altro paio	I can't see very well with these glasses, so I'll have to buy another pair (of them)
Le dispiacerebbe parlare un po' più forte? Non ci sento bene	Would you mind speaking louder? I can't hear very well

Ci is used with the verb *volere*: volerci means *to take* (time), *to be necessary* and in this case the subject is not expressed.
Volerci is used in the third person singular or in the third person plural depending upon the number of the noun (object) it precedes. In compound tenses the auxiliary is essere.

Per salire sull'autobus ci vuole il biglietto	To get on the bus you must (it is necessary) have a ticket
Ci vuole un'ora per andare in centro a piedi	It takes an hour to walk downtown
Ci vogliono dieci minuti per finire questo lavoro	It will take ten minutes to finish this job
C'è voluta un'ora per finire l'esercizio	It took one hour to finish the exercise

> NOTE *Meaning* to take *(time)* or *to be necessary* *when the subject is expressed, the verb* metterci *is used.*
>
> | | |
> |---|---|
> | *Per andare da Roma a Firenze ci vogliono due ore, ma io con la vecchia 'Panda' ci metto anche quattro ore* | *It takes two hours to drive from Rome to Florence, but with my old 'Panda' it takes me as long as four* |

NE, p. 311

Ne as a partitive pronoun (in English corresponds to *some of it, some of them, any of it, any of them*) is used for quantities and it is often introduced by the interrogative adjective quanto, quanta, quanti, quante.

■ Quante lezioni hai oggi? ● Ne ho tre	■ How many classes do you have today? ● I have three (of them)
Ho preso una bottiglia di vino e ne ho bevuto un bicchiere	I got a bottle of wine and I drank a glass (of it)

NOTE *Ne cannot be omitted and when it is used in a sentence with a compound tense, the past participle agrees in gender and number with the noun replaced by* ne
Ne precedes the verbs and in a negative sentence is placed after **non** *Combined with another pronoun it is in second position.*

■ *Quante cartoline hai scritto a Giorgio?*   ■ *How many postcards did you write to Giorgio?*
● *Non glie*ne *ho scritta nessuna*   ● *I didn't write (to) him any (of them)*

Ne as a pronoun replaces prepositional phrases introduced by the preposition **di** (*di questa/quella cosa-di questa/quella persona*) even when they are unexpressed, but implicit.

È un'attrice famosa, **ne** (di questa persona) parlano tutti	She is a famous actress, everybody talks about her

Ne is used after verbs followed by the preposition **di** such as **avere bisogno di** (*to need*), **valere la pena di** (*to be worth*), **non poterne più di** (*to be tired of, to be unable to resist*).

Non ho preso la macchina perché non **ne** avevo bisogno	I didn't use the car because I didn't need it
Basta torno a casa, non **ne** posso più di stare qui!	That's enough, I'm returning home, I'm tired of staying here!
Non visitare quel museo: non **ne** vale la pena!	Don't visit that museum, it's not worth visiting it!

Ne is used also as an adverb meaning *from that/this place*, with reference to a previously mentioned place.

È entrato in casa e **ne** è uscito dopo qualche minuto	He arrived home and left (from there) after a few minutes

The verb **andarsene** means *to go away* (from a place).

Non ne posso più di stare qui, **me ne vado**	I can't stay here anymore, I'm leaving
Non voglio più vederti: **vattene**!	I don't want to see you anymore: go away!
Non La voglio più vedere: **se ne vada**!	I don't want to see you anymore: go away!

PASSATO REMOTO, pp. 321-322-333

The passato remoto (*simple past*) is a simple tense. The regular conjugation for the *passato remoto* is formed adding the appropriate endings to the stem of the verb.
Verbs with an irregular conjugation (mostly second conjugation verbs) have irregular forms only in the first and third singular and in the third plural forms.
There is also a group of verbs completely irregular as the verb essere or the verb avere.

The passato remoto expresses an action developed and completed in the past (as the *passato prossimo*), but here the action has no continuing effect in the present (for the person speaking).

A vent'anni andai a New York, negli Stati Uniti	When I was twenty I went to New York, in the USA
Quella sera bevvi solo un bicchiere di birra	That night I drank only one beer

> **NOTE** *In the spoken language the passato prossimo is commonly used specially in the North of Italy, whereas in the South of Italy the passato remoto is largely used.*

NOMI MASCHILI IN -*A* - NOMI IN -*ISTA*, p. 332

Certain masculine nouns ending in -a have the regular masculine plural in -i.

il problema	the problem
i problemi	the problems
il programma	the program
i programmi	the programs

Nouns ending in -ista have both genders, masculine and/or feminine, depending on the person to whom they refer, they have appropriate plural forms.

il giornalista	the journalist
la giornalista	the journalist
i giornalisti	the journalists
le giornaliste	the journalists

I NOMI ALTERATI, pp. 325-333

Italian nouns can be altered to change the meaning slightly by adding different suffixes.

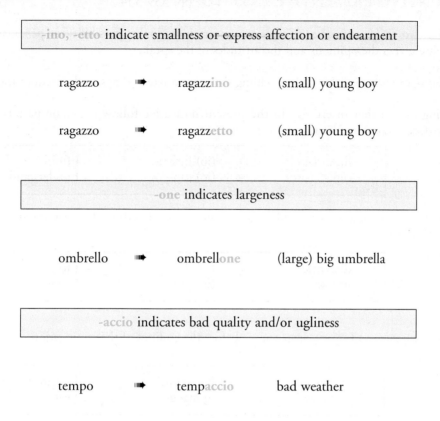

-ino, -etto indicate smallness or express affection or endearment

| ragazzo | ➠ | ragazzino | (small) young boy |
| ragazzo | ➠ | ragazzetto | (small) young boy |

-one indicates largeness

| ombrello | ➠ | ombrellone | (large) big umbrella |

-accio indicates bad quality and/or ugliness

| tempo | ➠ | tempaccio | bad weather |

CONGIUNTIVO PRESENTE E PASSATO, pp. 339-354

The **congiuntivo** (*subjunctive mood*) expresses uncertainty, doubt, possibility or personal feelings rather than facts. It conveys the opinions and the attitudes of the speaker.

The **congiuntivo presente** is formed by adding the appropriate endings to the stem of the verb.

Verbs ending in **-ire** that insert **-isc** in the present indicative follow the same pattern in the present subjunctive (see *Grammar Notes*, p. 6).

finire (-isc)	(io) finisca	I finish
capire (-isc)	(io) capisca	I understand

Verbs with infinitive ending in **-care** and **-gare** add an **-h-**, in all persons, between the stem and the present subjunctive endings.

dimenticare	(io) dimentichi	I forget
pagare	(io) paghi	I pay

Verbs ending in **-ciare** and **-giare** drop one **-i-** before the endings of the conjugation.

cominciare	io cominci	I begin
mangiare	io mangi	I eat

The following verbs have **irregular** present subjunctive forms (see p. 354).

andare	vada, vada, vada, andiamo, andiate, vadano
avere	abbia, abbia, abbia, abbiamo, abbiate, abbiano
capire	capisca, capisca, capisca, capiamo, capiate, capiscano
dare	dia, dia, dia, diamo, diate, diano
dire	dica, dica, dica, diciamo, diciate, dicano
dovere	debba, debba, debba, dobbiamo, dobbiate, debbano
essere	sia, sia, sia, siamo, siate, siano
fare	faccia, faccia, faccia, facciamo, facciate, facciano
potere	possa, possa, possa, possiamo, possiate, possano
sapere	sappia, sappia, sappia, sappiamo, sappiate, sappiano
sedersi	mi sieda, ti sieda, si sieda, ci sediamo, vi sediate, si siedano
stare	stia, stia, stia, stiamo, stiate, stiano
uscire	esca, esca, esca, usciamo, usciate, escano
venire	venga, venga, venga, veniamo, veniate, vengano
volere	voglia, voglia, voglia, vogliamo, vogliate, vogliano

> NOTE *With few exceptions the congiuntivo occurs only in subordinate clauses usually preceded by the conjunction che.*
> *Since (within each of the three conjugations) the singular endings are the same, singular subject pronouns are generally used to avoid confusion.*

The congiuntivo is introduced by verbs in the main clauses expressing opinions, wishes, doubts or volition (see p. 351). (When the subject of the main clause is the same as in the subordinate clause, the infinitive is required*)

Main clause	Subordinate clause	
Verbs expressing opinion		
Credo (I believe) Penso (I think) Immagino (I imagine) Suppongo (I suppose) Ritengo (I believe) Mi pare (it seems to me) Mi sembra (it seems to me)	che (that)	Carlo abbia ragione Carlo is right
	*di avere ragione	I am right

Main clause	Subordinate clause	
Verbs expressing emotion or state of mind		
Spero (I hope) Sono contento (I am happy) Mi auguro (I wish) Non vedo l'ora (I can't wait) Ho paura, temo (I fear) Mi dispiace (I am sorry)	che (that)	Carlo torni Carlo returns
	*di tornare	to come back

Main clause	Subordinate clause	
Verbs expressing volition/desire		
Voglio (I want) Desidero (I wish) Bisogna (it's necessary) È necessario (it's necessary)	che (that)	Carlo studi di più Carlo studies more
	*studiare di più	to study more

> NOTE *The English construction* "they want me to go to Italy" *in Italian is rendered as:* "vogliono che io vada in Italia".

The congiuntivo is also introduced by impersonal expressions (when the subject is not expressed, an infinitive follows*):

È meglio (it's better) È bene (it's good) È un peccato (it's a pity) È possibile (it's possible)	che (that)	Carlo non vada alla festa Carlo doesn't go to the party

*È meglio (it's better) *È possibile (it's possible)	*non andare alla festa not to go to the party

> NOTE *The expression* può darsi/è probabile *(may be, it is likely), is always followed by a subjunctive. It has an equivalent adverb* forse, *which is always followed by the indicative.*
>
> *Può darsi che* Maria *venga* alla festa   *Mary may come to the party*
> *Forse* Maria *viene* alla festa   *Perhaps Mary will come to the party*
>
> Secondo me, per me *(in my opinion/according to me) are followed by the indicative (see p. 340)*
>
> *Secondo me è* meglio viaggiare   *In my opinion it is better to use*
> *con i mezzi pubblici*   *public transportation*

The congiuntivo is also introduced by some conjunctions (see pp. 349-350).

1. Prima che (*before*)

Vado a trovare Michele prima che (lui) parta   I am going to visit Michele before he leaves

> NOTE *Prima is followed by the preposition* di + infinitive *when the subject is the same in both clauses.*
>
> *Vado a trovare Michele* prima di partire   *I am going to visit Michele before leaving*

2. Purché, a patto che, a condizione che (*provided that, on the condition that*)

Ci vengo volentieri   I'll be happy to go there
purché non ci sia Alberto   on the condition that Alberto is not there

3. Benché, sebbene, quantunque (*although, in spite of, even though*)

Esco di casa benché faccia freddo   I'm going out even though it is cold

4. Affinché, perché (*in order to, in order that, so that*)

Scrivo a Marta **perché sappia** come stanno le cose	I'm writing to Marta so that she knows how things are going

In order to, in order that, so that can also be expressed by per + infinitive.

Scrivo a Marta **per informarla** del mio progetto	I'm writing to Marta in order to inform her about my plan

> **NOTE** *When the subject of the two clauses is the same,* di + infinitive *is used (see p. 339).*
>
> | | | |
> |---|---|---|
> | *Carlo pensa* *Carlo thinks* | *di essere* *he is* | *intelligente* *intelligent* |
> | *Carlo crede* *Carlo believes* | *di avere* *he is* | *ragione* *right* |
>
> *If the infinitive depends on the verbs* volere, preferire, desiderare *the preposition* di *is not used.*
>
> | | | | |
> |---|---|---|---|
> | *Carlo* | *vuole* *preferisce* *desidera* | *wants* *prefers* *wishes* | *tornare presto* to come back soon |

CONGIUNTIVO PASSATO, pp. 339-354

The congiuntivo passato is formed with the present subjunctive of the auxiliary verbs avere or essere + the past participle of the main verb.

Because of the relationship between the two clauses, the tenses of the subjunctive are determined by the tense of the main clause on which the subjunctive depends. When the verb of the main clause is in the present tense, it is followed by present subjunctive, or simple future, or past subjunctive (see pp. 351-352).

Main clause		Subordinate clause	
(adesso)	Penso che (*presente indicativo*) I think that	(dopo)	piova (*presente congiuntivo*) it is going to rain pioverà (*futuro semplice*) it will rain
		(adesso)	piova (*presente congiuntivo*) it is raining
		(prima)	sia piovuto (*passato congiuntivo*) it has been raining

FORMA IMPERSONALE, pp. 353-354

The Italian **forma impersonale** corresponds to the English impersonal construction introduced by *one, we, people, they…*
The Italian construction is formed by **si + the third person singular of the verb**.

Con "Radio Libera" **si lavora**	With "Radio Libera" one works
Spesso **si parla** bene e **si agisce** male	When people speak correctly, they frequently act incorrectly

The impersonal construction with **reflexive verbs** is made by using the pronoun combination **ci si**

Con "Radio Libera" **ci si diverte**	With "Radio Libera" you have fun
e **ci si informa**	and you are informed

CONGIUNTIVO IMPERFETTO E TRAPASSATO, pp. 360-361-373-382

Like the *congiuntivo presente* and *passato* the **congiuntivo imperfetto e trapassato** express uncertainty, doubt, possibility.

The *congiuntivo imperfetto* is made by adding the appropriate endings to the verb stem (see pp. 360-361).

The following verbs have **irregular** forms.

bere	bevessi, bevessi, bevesse, bevessimo, beveste, bevessero
dare	dessi, dessi, desse, dessimo, deste, dessero
dire	dicessi, dicessi, dicesse, dicessimo, diceste, dicessero
essere	fossi, fossi, fosse, fossimo, foste, fossero
fare	facessi, facessi, facesse, facessimo, faceste, facessero
stare	stessi, stessi, stesse, stessimo, steste, stessero
tradurre	traducessi, traducessi, traducesse, traducessimo, traduceste, traducessero

As with the *congiuntivo presente*, the **congiuntivo imperfetto** is introduced **in the main clause** by:

a) verbs of **opinion, volition/desire, emotion** and **state of mind** (see *Grammar Notes*, Unità 16) **in the past tense or in the present conditional**

Carlo **pensava** che (loro) **fossero** a casa   Carlo thought that they were at home

Vorrei che (tu) **cercassi** un buon lavoro   I'd like you to look for a good job

> **NOTE** *Present conditional in the main clause followed by imperfect subjunctive are used **to express desire-wish** (see p. 369).*
>
> *Il mio uomo ideale…: **vorrei che fosse** biondo e **avesse** gli occhi azzurri*   *My ideal man… I would like him to be blond and to have blue eyes*

b) **impersonal expressions** (see Unità 16) **in the past tense and in the conditional**

Era meglio che Carlo **andasse** alla festa   It was better that Carlo went to the party

Sarebbe meglio che lei **andasse** alla festa   It would be better if she went to the party

c) **conjunctions** (see Unità 16).

1. Prima che (*before*)

Sono andato a trovare Michele	I visited Michele
prima che partisse	before he left

> NOTE *Prima is followed by the preposition di + infinitive when the subject is the same in both clause.*
>
> *Sono andato a trovare Michele* I visited Michele
> *prima di partire* before leaving

2. Purché, a patto che, a condizione che/di (*provided that, on the condition that*)

Ho accettato l'invito	I accepted the invitation
purché non ci **fosse** Gino	provided that Gino didn't come

3. Benché, sebbene, nonostante che (*although, in spite of, even though*)

Benché facesse freddo sono uscita di casa	I went out even though it was cold

4. Affinché, perché (*in order to, in order that, so that*)

Ho scritto a Giovanna **perché**	I wrote to Giovanna (in order) to ask her
mi **prenotasse** una camera in albergo	to book a room for me in a hotel

In order to/that, **so that** can also be expressed by **per + infinitive**

Ho scritto a Giovanna **per invitarla**	I wrote to Giovanna (in order) to invite her
al mio matrimonio	to my wedding

> NOTE *When the subject of both, the main and subordinate clauses is the same, di + the infinitive is used. If the infinitive depends on the verbs volere, preferire or desiderare the preposition di is not used.*
>
> *Carlo pensava di essere in ritardo* Carlo thought he was late
>
> *Carlo voleva partire subito* Carlo wanted to leave immediately

CONGIUNTIVO TRAPASSATO, pp. 361-382

The **congiuntivo trapassato** is formed with the **imperfect subjunctive** of **avere** and **essere + the past participle of the verb**
It is used when the verb in the main clause is in the past tense, and the action in the subordinate happens before the action in the main clause.

Carlo pensava che avessi già mangiato   Carlo thought that I had already eaten

Carlo credeva che fossero già partiti   Carlo thought that they had already left

When the verb of the main clause is in the past tense or in the conditional it is followed by **imperfect subjunctive**, or **pluperfect subjunctive**, or **past conditional** (see p. 374).

Main clause		Subordinate clause	
(ieri) Pensavo *(passato indicativo)* Ho pensato I thought	che that	(dopo)	sarebbe piovuto *(condizionale composto)* it would rain
		(ora)	piovesse *(imperfetto congiuntivo)* it was raining
Vorrei *(condizionale presente)* I would like I wish		(prima)	fosse piovuto *(trapassato congiuntivo)* it had rained

> **NOTE** *The past conditional in the subordinate clause expresses a future action related to the past action of the main clause.*
>
> *(ieri) Pensavo che (oggi) sarebbe piovuto*   *(yesterday) I thought it would rain (today)*

PERIODO IPOTETICO, pp. 380-382

Hypothetical statements are always made up of two clauses:

a) the *if clause*, that is the subordinate clause that starts with se (*if*);
b) the *result clause*, that is the main clause.

There are three types of *if*-clauses:

1. hypothesis with conviction and certainty

> Se + presente indicativo + presente indicativo

Se finisco di lavorare presto, vengo a trovarti   If I finish work early, I will come to visit you

> Se + futuro indicativo + futuro indicativo

Se finirò di lavorare presto verrò a trovarti   If I finish work early, I will come to visit you

Se + presente indicativo + imperativo

Se **hai bisogno** di me, **telefonami**!   If you need me, call me!

2. hypothetical condition unlikely to happen.

Se + congiuntivo imperfetto + condizionale presente

Se **finissi** di lavorare presto **verrei** a trovarti   If I finished work early, I would come to visit you

3. hypothetical condition in the past that did not materialize.

Se + congiuntivo trapassato + condizionale composto

Se **avessi finito** di lavorare presto ieri sera, **sarei venuto** a trovarti   If I had finished work early last night, I would have come to visit you

> **NOTE** *Se never introduces a verb in the conditional form.*
> *In hypothetical statements you can switch the order of the main clause and the subordinate clause.*
>
> *Se finisco di lavorare presto vengo a trovarti*
> *or*
> *Vengo a trovarti se finisco di lavorare presto*

The idiomatic expression **magari + imperfect or pluperfect subjunctive** emphatizes wish/desire (see pp. 369-382).

Magari vincessi al Superenalotto!   I wish I could win Superenalotto!

Magari avessi **vinto** al Superenalotto!   I wish I had won Superenalotto!

FORMA PASSIVA, pp. 388-389-393-396

The **forma passiva** (*passive voice*) expresses an action performed on the subject. It is formed, as it is in English, by using the verb **essere** (or **venire**) **+ the past participle** of the main verb which must agree in gender and number with the subject of the sentence.

An active sentence can be turned into the passive just as in English.

La Fiat **fabbrica** la "Punto"	Fiat produces the "Punto" car
La "Punto" **è fabbricata** dalla Fiat	The "Punto" car is produced by Fiat

In the passive voice the direct object of the active sentence becomes the subject and the subject of the original sentence is the agent preceded by the preposition **da** (*by*).

NOTE   *To form the passive, the auxiliary* **venire** *is often used instead of the auxiliary* essere *but only with non compound tenses.*

La "Punto"	è (viene)	fabbricata	dalla Fiat
The "Punto" car	is	produced	by Fiat
Anche la "500"	era (veniva)*	fabbricata	dalla Fiat
The "500" car	was also	produced	by Fiat
Una nuova macchina	sarà (verrà)*	fabbricata	dalla Fiat
A new car	will be	produced	by Fiat
Un uomo	è stato	ucciso	da un rapinatore
A man	was	killed	by a robber
I ladri	sono stati	arrestati	dalla polizia
The robbers	were	arrested	by the police

* *Venire is used only with non compound tenses.*

SI PASSIVANTE, pp. 393-396

The *si* **passivante** is made up of **si + third person singular or plural** of the verbs in all tenses and often replaces passive structures where an agent is not expressed.

Il parmigiano reggiano si produce | Parmisan cheese is produced
in Emilia Romagna | in Emilia Romagna

I tortellini si producono | Tortellini are produced
in Emilia Romagna | in Emilia Romagna

The above sentences are equivalent to the passive sentences:

Il parmigiano reggiano è prodotto in Emilia Romagna
Il parmigiano reggiano viene prodotto in Emilia Romagna

I tortellini sono prodotti in Emilia Romagna
I tortellini vengono prodotti in Emilia Romagna

In Italian there is an idiomatic use of the verb andare instead of *essere* (only with non-compound verbs) in the third person singular and plural + past participle of the verb which agrees in gender and number with the subject. It indicates obligation and necessity in an impersonal way (see pp. 393-396).

Il parmigiano reggiano | Parmisan cheese
va conservato in un luogo fresco | must be kept in a cool place

I tortellini vanno cotti | Tortellini must be cooked
in molta acqua salata | in a lot of salted water

Equivalent ways to express necessity are:

Il parmigiano reggiano si deve conservare
in un luogo fresco
Il parmigiano reggiano deve essere | Parmisan cheese must be kept in a cool place
conservato in un luogo fresco

I tortellini si devono cuocere
in molta acqua salata
I tortellini devono essere cotti | Tortellini must be cooked in a lot of salted water
in molta acqua salata

GERUNDIO - INFINITO - PARTICIPIO, pp. 404-412-414-415

The **gerundio** expresses an action or state of being that accompanies the action of the main verb.
The **gerundio semplice** (*simple gerund*) is formed by adding the endings to the stem of the verb and it is invariable.

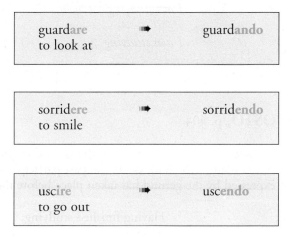

guard**are** to look at	⟹	guard**ando**
sorrid**ere** to smile	⟹	sorrid**endo**
usc**ire** to go out	⟹	usc**endo**

The *gerundio* is equivalent to a subordinate clause expressing time, manner or cause.

The actions of the main and the subordinate clauses take place **at the same time** and the *gerundio* refers to the subject of the main clause (see p. 404).

Aspettando l'autobus (io) leggo sempre il giornale	I always read the newspaper while waiting for the bus
(voi) Avete incontrato Eugenio **uscendo** di casa	You met Eugenio while you were leaving your house

The *gerundio* is used as:

a) **valore di tempo** (time-coincidence) (see p. 404).

Pensando ai suoi problemi Antonio fuma una sigaretta dopo l'altra = Mentre (Antonio) pensa ai suoi problemi, Antonio fuma una sigaretta dopo l'altra	Antonio smokes one cigarette after another, while thinking of his problems

b) **valore di causa** (cause or reason) (see p. 404).

Non **dovendo lavorare** (io) esco = Poiché (io) non devo lavorare esco	Since I don't have to work I go out

c) **valore di modo** (way or manner) (see p. 404).

Paolo ha passato il fine settimana **studiando**   Paolo spent the week-end studying

> **NOTE** *To express emphatically an action in progress in the present or in the past you can use the gerundio semplice* preceded by the present or imperfect indicative of the verb stare.
>
> *Sto studiando*   *I am studying*
>
> *Stavo studiando*   *I was studying*

GERUNDIO COMPOSTO, p. 404

The **gerundio composto** (*compound gerund*) is formed by the gerund of the auxiliary verbs **avere** and **essere + the past participle** of the main verb. With essere the past participle agrees with the subject.
It is used when the action expressed by the gerund has taken place before the action of the main verb.

Avendo finito di studiare,   Having finished studying,
(noi) usciamo di casa   we go out

Essendo uscita presto di casa,   Having left home early,
(lei) arrivò alla stazione in anticipo   she arrived at the station early

> **NOTE** *Direct, indirect and reflexive pronouns are attached to the end of the* gerundio semplice; *in the* gerundio composto *they are attached to the auxiliaries.*
>
> *Guardandola le sorridevo*   *Looking at her I was smiling*
>
> *Essendomi svegliato tardi,*   *Having woken up late,*
> *ho perso il treno*   *I missed the train*

INFINITO SEMPLICE, p. 415

The **infinito semplice** (*simple infinitive*) is the unconjugated form of a verb (in English *to + the verb*). The simple infinitive expresses an action contemporary to the main clause no matter the tense of the verb of the main clause.
It has three conjugations.

am**are**	scriv**ere**	part**ire**
to love	to write	to leave

The infinitive is used in Italian as an English gerund:

a) **as subject of a sentence**

Fumare non fa bene alla salute   Smoking is not good for the health

b) **as object of certain verbs**:
volere, potere, dovere, sapere, amare, desiderare, fare, piacere, preferire…

Amo viaggiare   I like travelling

Preferiscono mangiare pesce   ʻ   They prefer eating fish

c) **after some prepositions**

Un signore di Roma andava a fare   A man from Rome used to do
un po' di jogging   some jogging

Most verbs require a preposition before an infinitive.

Here is a list of the most common verbs + prepositions.

abituarsi a	to get used to
andare a	to go
cominciare a	to begin
continuare a	to continue
imparare a	to learn
insegnare a	to teach
pensare a	to think of/about
provare a	to try
riuscire a	to succeed
accettare di	to accept
accorgersi di	to notice
avere bisogno di	to need
avere intenzione di	to intend
avere paura di	to be afraid
avere voglia di	to feel like
decidere di	to decide
finire di	to finish
pensare di	to plan
promettere di	to promise
contare su	to count on
riflettere su	to ponder on
scommettere su	to bet on
derivare da	to derive from
dipendere da	to depend on

d) **after expressions** such as:

Prima di

Ogni mattina **prima di andare** in ufficio,
il signore andava a Villa Borghese

Before going to the office
the man used to go to the Villa Borghese every morning

Senza

Senza dire una parola è uscito

Without saying a word he went out

Invece di

Invece di studiare è uscita

Instead of studying she went out

INFINITO COMPOSTO, pp. 412-415

The **infinito composto** (*compound infinitive*) is made up of **avere** or **essere + the past participle** of the verb.
The **infinito composto** is used to express an action that has taken place before the action expressed in the main clause, no matter the tense of the verb of the main clause. It must always be used after **dopo**.
Usually the *-e* of *avere* drops in front of the past participle.

Dopo aver studiato esco
= Dopo che ho studiato esco

After studying I go out

Dopo essere tornata a casa
Maria ha guardato la TV
= Dopo che è ritornata a casa
Maria ha guardato la TV

After returning home Mary watched TV

NOTE *Direct, indirect and reflexive pronouns must be attached to the end of the* infinito semplice *and in the* infinito composto *to the end of the auxiliaries.*

Ho bisogno di parlarti

I need to speak to you

Dopo essermi vestito esco

After getting dressed I go out

PARTICIPIO PRESENTE, p. 415

The **participio presente** (*present participle*) may be the equivalent of the relative clause.
It is formed by adding **-ante** to the stem of **-are** verbs, **-ente** to the stem of **-ere** and **-ire** verbs.

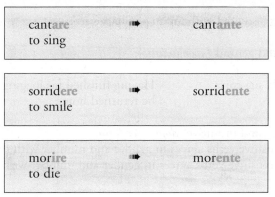

It is used:

a) **as an adjective**
It agrees with the noun it modifies.

Ho visto molte facce **sorridenti**   I saw many smiling faces

b) **as a noun**
It takes the definite or the indefinite article.

Ho conosciuto un **cantante** famoso   I met a famous singer

Gli **studenti** sono arrivati ieri   The students arrived yesterday

PARTICIPIO PASSATO, p. 415

The **participio passato** (*past participle*) is formed by adding **-ato** to the stem of **-are** verbs, **-uto** to the stem of **-ere** verbs, and **-ito** to the stem of **-ire** verbs.

> The **participio passato** is usually combined with the auxiliary verbs *essere* and *avere* to form compound tenses.

The **participio passato** is also used without an auxiliary verb:

a) instead of the compound gerund *(avendo fatto)*;

Finita (= avendo finito) la sua corsa l'uomo tornò a casa	Having finished his jogging he returned home

b) *instead* of *dopo* + compound infinitive *(dopo aver fatto)*.
The past participle of transitive verbs agrees in gender and number with the object.
The past participle of intransitive verbs agrees in gender and number with the subject.

Fatta (= avendo fatto) **la barba** un uomo dovrebbe sentirsi già in forma	Having shaved, a man, should feel in good shape
Fatti (= avendo fatto) **i** compiti i bambini sono usciti	Having done their homework, the children went out
Fatte (= avendo fatto) **le** vacanze le persone si sentono meglio	Having had holidays, people feel better
Arrivata (= dopo essere arrivata) a casa, Luisa ha cenato	Having arrived at home, Luisa had her dinner

As in English the past participle may be placed at the very beginning of the sentence (see p. 414).

Dopo che avrò fatto **Dopo aver fatto** **Avendo fatto** **Fatto**	l'esame	andrò al mare
Having done	the exam	I'll go to the seaside